First World War
and Army of Occupation
War Diary
France, Belgium and Germany

35 DIVISION
105 Infantry Brigade
Prince of Wales's (North Staffordshire Regiment)
4th Battalion
6 October 1917 - 24 April 1919

WO95/2488/3

The Naval & Military Press Ltd
www.nmarchive.com
Published in association with The National Archives

Published by

The Naval & Military Press Ltd

Unit 10 Ridgewood Industrial Park,

Uckfield, East Sussex,

TN22 5QE England

Tel: +44 (0) 1825 749494

www.naval-military-press.com

www.nmarchive.com

This diary has been reprinted in facsimile from the original. Any imperfections are inevitably reproduced and the quality may fall short of modern type and cartographic standards.

© Crown Copyright
Images reproduced by permission of The National Archives, London, England, 2015.

Contents

Document type	Place/Title	Date From	Date To
Heading	WO95/2488/3 4 Battalion North Staffordshire Regiment		
Heading	35th Division 105th Infy Bde 4th Bn North Stafford Regt 1917 Oct-Apr 1919.		
Heading	35th Division 106th Infy Bde 105 Bde 4th Bn Nth Staffords Oct 1917-Jan 1918		
War Diary		06/10/1917	15/10/1917
War Diary		14/10/1917	31/10/1917
Miscellaneous	To:- D.A.G. 3rd Echelon.	05/12/1917	05/12/1917
War Diary		01/11/1917	30/11/1917
Operation(al) Order(s)	Operation Order No. 132.	29/11/1917	29/11/1917
War Diary		01/12/1917	30/01/1918
Heading	105th Inf. Bde. 35th Div. War Diary 4th Battn. The North Staffordshire Regiment. February March 1918		
War Diary	In the Field	01/02/1918	01/03/1918
War Diary	Canal Bank North.	03/03/1918	11/03/1918
War Diary		10/03/1918	10/03/1918
War Diary	Zuidhuis Camp.	11/03/1918	22/03/1918
War Diary		12/03/1918	21/03/1918
War Diary	Zuidhuis Camp.	23/03/1918	23/03/1918
War Diary	Mericourt L'Abbe	24/03/1918	24/03/1918
War Diary	Maricourt.	24/03/1918	26/03/1918
War Diary	Buire.	26/03/1918	31/03/1918
War Diary	La Houssoye	01/04/1918	30/04/1918
War Diary	Bouzincourt	01/05/1918	02/05/1918
War Diary	Herissart	03/05/1918	15/05/1918
War Diary		08/05/1918	15/05/1918
War Diary	Bank V.8.b.	16/05/1918	19/05/1918
War Diary		17/05/1918	20/05/1918
War Diary	Line	20/05/1918	23/05/1918
War Diary	Line Bouzincourt	23/05/1918	31/05/1918
War Diary	Bouzincourt	01/06/1918	04/06/1918
War Diary	Hedauville	05/06/1918	10/06/1918
War Diary	Bouzincourt	11/06/1918	12/06/1918
War Diary	Hedauville	13/06/1918	16/06/1918
War Diary	Beauquesne	17/06/1918	23/06/1918
War Diary	Puchvillers	24/06/1918	29/06/1918
War Diary	Candas.	30/06/1918	30/06/1918
War Diary	Wizernes.	01/07/1918	04/07/1918
War Diary	Mont Rouge	05/07/1918	09/07/1918
War Diary		07/07/1918	31/07/1918
War Diary	In the field	01/08/1918	06/08/1918
War Diary	Boeschepe.	07/08/1918	08/08/1918
War Diary	Near St. Silvestre Cappel.	08/08/1918	14/08/1918
War Diary	St. Silvestre Cappel	15/08/1918	15/08/1918
War Diary	In the Field.	15/08/1918	25/08/1918
War Diary	St. Silvestre Cappel.	25/08/1918	30/08/1918
War Diary	Boeschepe.	30/08/1918	31/08/1918
War Diary	St. Silvestre.	01/09/1918	30/09/1918
War Diary	Tenbrielen	01/10/1918	31/10/1918
War Diary	Sweveghem	01/11/1918	01/11/1918

War Diary	Marcke	02/11/1918	07/11/1918
War Diary	Courtrai	08/11/1918	09/11/1918
War Diary	Ingoyghem	10/11/1918	10/11/1918
War Diary	Pensemont	11/11/1918	13/11/1918
War Diary	Renaix	14/11/1918	20/11/1918
War Diary	Heule	20/11/1918	28/11/1918
War Diary	Gheluwe	29/11/1918	29/11/1918
War Diary	Poperinghe	30/11/1918	30/11/1918
War Diary	Terdeghem	01/12/1918	01/12/1918
War Diary	Wulverdinghe	02/12/1918	02/12/1918
War Diary	Bayenghem	02/12/1918	09/12/1918
War Diary	Nortleulinghem	10/12/1918	28/01/1919
War Diary	Calais	29/01/1919	05/02/1919
War Diary	Les Bardes	06/02/1919	05/03/1919
War Diary	Beaumaris	06/03/1919	25/03/1919
War Diary	Nortleulinghem	26/03/1919	31/03/1919
Miscellaneous	4th N. Stafford Regt.	26/04/1919	26/04/1919
War Diary	Nortleulinghem	01/04/1919	24/04/1919

20/45/2468/3

4 Battalion North Staffordshire Regiment.

35TH DIVISION
105TH INFY BDE

4TH BN NORTH STAFFORD REGT
1917 OCT ~~FEB 1918~~-APR 1919

From UK

35TH DIVISION
Attached 106TH INFY BDE

105 BDE

4TH BN NTH STAFFORDS
OCT 1917 - JAN 1918

WAR DIARY
INTELLIGENCE SUMMARY.
(Erase heading not required.)

Hour, Date, Place	Summary of Events and Information	Remarks and references to Appendices
6th October 1914	3 A.M. 4 Officers and 84 other ranks and complete transport entrained at Canterbury West and proceeded to Southampton. 7.35 A.M. C.O., Adjt. and 22 Officers + 680 other ranks entrained at Canterbury East and proceeded to Southampton. 10.30 A.M. 2 n.c.o. in command, 1 Sergt. Adjt., 14 Officers and 40 other ranks entrained at Canterbury East and proceeded to Southampton. 5. P.M. 4 Officers and 84 other ranks and transport sailed for Havre. 1.0 P.M. C.O. and 34 Officers and 908 other ranks sailed for Havre.	
7th October 1914	8 A.M. C.O. and 34 Officers and 908 other ranks landed at Havre and proceeded to No 2 Rest Camp 5. wrote Order. 4 other ranks to hospital off strength. 8 P.M. 4 Officers and 84 other ranks and transport landed at Havre and proceeded to No 2 Rest Camp to await Orders.	
8th October 1914		

4 N 36 Offrs
106/35
W F I

WAR DIARY
or
INTELLIGENCE SUMMARY.
(Erase heading not required.)

Army Form C. 2118.

Hour, Date, Place	Summary of Events and Information	Remarks and references to Appendices
8th October 1917	1 other rank to hospital off strength.	
9th October 1917	Nil.	
10th October 1917	3 p.m. Sgt Day C.M.G. proceeded to 3rd Echelon on duty. 10. p.m. C.O. & 43 officers 98 & other ranks entrained at Nauroi	
11th October 1917	The battalion detrained at Bapaume at 12 noon. marched to field at Frencourt and erected Camp at 4.30 p.m. (I.14. C.8.x) M.F.5 C.N.W. and attached to 56th Division.	
12th October 1917	C.O. and Adjt reconnoitred arrangements for attachment and visited 167th, 168th & 169th Brigades. 1 other rank to C.C.S. off strength.	
13 October 1917	C.O. and Adjt attached to H.Q. 9th Bgd.	

Army Form C. 2118.

WAR DIARY
or
INTELLIGENCE SUMMARY.
(Erase heading not required.)

Instructions regarding War Diaries and Intelligence Summaries are contained in F.S. Regs., Part II. and the Staff Manual respectively. Title pages will be prepared in manuscript.

Hour, Date, Place	Summary of Events and Information	Remarks and references to Appendices
13th October 1917 (contd)	Battalion of 169th Inf. Bde (4th Middlesex Regt.)	
	"A" Coy attached 1st London Regt 167th Bde.	
	"B" Coy " " 1st Middlesex Regt " "	
	"C" Coy " " 12th London Regt. 168th Bde	
	"D" Coy " " G.W.R. Regt. 169th Bde.	
13th 15th October 1917	Individual training in trench work.	
14th October 1917	Signalling Officers attached to 4th Middlesex Regt.	⟨⟩
15th October 1917	Section training in the line	⟨⟩
16th October 1917	2nd in Command, Staff Offr and 3 gun officers attached to 5th Middlesex Regt in the line.	
	1 other rank wounded in action.	
	1 " " killed " "	
	1 " " " "	
16th October 1917	Battalion in reserve to Trentcourt.	⟨⟩
	1st out training.	
	2 other ranks accidentally wounded.	

Army Form C. 2118.

WAR DIARY
or
INTELLIGENCE SUMMARY.
(Erase heading not required.)

Instructions regarding War Diaries and Intelligence Summaries are contained in F. S. Regs., Part II. and the Staff Manual respectively. Title pages will be prepared in manuscript.

Hour, Date, Place	Summary of Events and Information	Remarks and references to Appendices
19th October 1917	1 other rank to C.C.S. off strength.	"
20th October 1917	2 " " " "	"
21st October 1917	Nil.	"
22nd October 1917	One division moved into the trenches for training as follows.	"
	A Coy attached to 8th Middlesex Regt.	
	B Coy " " 3rd London Regt.	
	C Coy " " Rangers Regt.	
	D Coy " " Q.V.R. Regt.	
	For platoon and company training.	
23rd October 1917	Nil	
24th October 1917	1 other rank to C.C.S. off strength	"
25th October 1917	C.O. and 2nd in Command inspected "D" Coy in the line and returned the same day.	"

WAR DIARY
or
INTELLIGENCE SUMMARY.
(Erase heading not required.)

Army Form C. 2118.

Hour, Date, Place	Summary of Events and Information	Remarks and references to Appendices
26th October 1917	O.C. 2nd in Command & Adjt. worked B' Coy in the line to inspect training.	N
27th October 1917	O.C. inspected A & B. Coys in the line to see the result of bombances working as such.	N
28th October 1917	Battalion returns to Frencourt for rest and training.	N
29th October 1917	O.C's inspection of camp, and a general clean-up of the men.	N
30th October 1917	Progressive training of the Companies.	N
31st October 1917	Route march around Bavincourt, in order to show the men the battalion by the enemy.	N

To:- D.A.G.

    3rd Echelon.

    Herewith War Diary for month of November.

5th Decr 1917.　　　　W.Appleyard　　　　Lieut Colonel.

    Commanding 4th Bn. North Staffordshire Regt.

35

4 N Staff GI Army Form C. 2118.

Vol II

WAR DIARY
or
INTELLIGENCE SUMMARY.
(Erase heading not required.)

Instructions regarding War Diaries and Intelligence Summaries are contained in F.S. Regs., Part II. and the Staff Manual respectively. Title pages will be prepared in manuscript.

Hour, Date, Place	Summary of Events and Information	Remarks and references to Appendices
4th Nov 1917	Proceeded to front line trenches Hyacinth	
4th Nov 1917	PRONVILLE.	
	No 40403 L/Cpl Baxter, killed in action "D" Coy.	
	" 32618 " " " wounded (shellshock) " "	
	" 45007 " " " " " " D Coy.	
	2 L.T.M.B. scouts Missing (did not return from patrol).	
	Cpl. No 30141 L/Cpl Whelay " "	
	No 48494 Pte Whittaker killed in action B "	
	" 48563 " Land wounded " "	
	" 38329 " Lunn " "	
	" 42533 " Wilson " "	
6th Nov 1917	Return to Camp at FREMICOURT.	
9th Nov 1917	Left FREMICOURT by motor bus via BAPAUME-BOYELLES-ARRAS. Billeted for one night	

79/3208

Army Form C. 2118.

WAR DIARY
or
INTELLIGENCE SUMMARY.
(Erase heading not required.)

Instructions regarding War Diaries and Intelligence Summaries are contained in F.S. Regs., Part II. and the Staff Manual respectively. Title pages will be prepared in manuscript.

Hour, Date, Place	Summary of Events and Information	Remarks and references to Appendices
10th Nov 1914	Proceeded by motor bus via CAMBLAIN L'ABBÉ - ESTREE-CAUCHIE RANCHICOURT-HOUDAIN - BRUAY. Billeted for one night.	
11th Nov 1914	By motor bus via MARLES-LES-MINES - LILLERS - ST. HILAIRE-AIRE - THIENNES.	
12th Nov 1914	Billeted at THIENNES. (rested)	
13th Nov 1914	" " (route march)	
14th Nov 1914	Marched via STEENBECQUE - HAZEBROUCK - ST. SYLVESTRE CAPPEL - STEENVORDE. Billeted for night.	
15th Nov 1914	Marched via ABEELE - POPERINGHE - VLAMERTINGHE to camp near CHATEAU DES TROIS TOURS. Joined 106th Brigade, 35th Division.	

Army Form C. 2118.

WAR DIARY
or
INTELLIGENCE SUMMARY.
(Erase heading not required.)

Instructions regarding War Diaries and Intelligence Summaries are contained in F.S. Regs., Part II. and the Staff Manual respectively. Title pages will be prepared in manuscript.

Hour, Date, Place	Summary of Events and Information	Remarks and references to Appendices
16th Nov 1914	Proceeded to YPRES in Brigade reserve in burst from E. of BRIELEN, 1½ miles N. of ST. JULIEN. Whole POE-CAPPELLE.	
17th Nov 1914	2/No 3+436 Sgt I. Worryell killed in action "B" " 3801 R Pte Vmais " " " "B" " 4039 " Seeep " " " "B" Lieut S.C. Noroey wounded Sgt Fenge No 2+666 " (and 3 wounds) "B" Cpl Eward No 3114 " " " "B" " Pield No 31810 " " " "B" Pte Vmais No 3+204 " " " "B" Ld Chippfields 4652 " " " "B" Pte Cones No 40361 " " " "B"	
21st Nov 1914	Returned to Divisional Reserve at YPRES Camp, situated on main Dranoy	

Army Form C. 2118.

WAR DIARY
or
INTELLIGENCE SUMMARY.
(Erase heading not required.)

Instructions regarding War Diaries and Intelligence Summaries are contained in F. S. Regs., Part II. and the Staff Manual respectively. Title pages will be prepared in manuscript.

Hour, Date, Place	Summary of Events and Information	Remarks and references to Appendices
22nd Nov 1917	Battalion inspected by Brigadier General L. W. Y. Sotheran C.M.G.	
23rd Nov 1917	Battalion inspected by Major General J. M. S. Lanks G.B.	
28th Nov 1917	Relieved the 10th Cheshire Regt as follows:- 2 Coys at KEMPTON PARK, 2 Coy VARNA FARM, 1 Coy CANAL BANK.	
29th Nov 1917	3 O.R. killed. 1 D. Boy 19 O.R. wounded.	
30th Nov 1917	3 O.R. wounded "D" Coy.	

SECRET   Copy No. 5

OPERATION ORDER No 132

Personnel of Half Co. 106th M.G. Co. will relieve
Personnel of Half Co. 106th M.G.C. in the Poelcappelle
Sector on night 30th Nov/1st Dec. 1917.

1. **DISPOSITIONS**
   All positions will be handed over as taken over.

2. **COMMAND**
   Left Sub-Sector 2/Lt H H Buckley   HQ V.14.c.1.1m.
   Centre Sub-Sector 2/Lt W.S. Whitehouse H.Q Gloster FM
   Right Sub-Sector 2/Lt J Seddon   H.Q Burns House.

3. **PARADE**
   Relieving personnel will parade at 2pm
   Dress, fighting order - Jerkins rolled on belt. One pair
   of socks will be carried on the man.
   1 Bottle whale oil will be carried per detachment.

4. **GUIDES** for Sect. H.Q will be at Kempton Park at
   1.30pm Guides for detachments at Sec HQ on arrival.

5. **RATIONS**
   2 days rations will be carried in addition to the
   unconsumed portion of the days rations.

6. **WATER**
                                                    of water
   Water bottles will be carried full. 1 Petrol tin per
   detachment & 1 per Sect HQ. will be carried to
   last the 2 days

7. **EQUIPMENT**
   Guns, Tripods, Belt boxes, Condenser bags and
   Tubes. S.A.A. Trench Stores, Schemes and Maps will
   be taken over

8. **T.P.Rs** will be rendered by each section
   to reach Co.HQ by 7.30AM daily

9. Completion of relief will be reported by
   word "KITTY" to this office

   _____

   Issued at 6.55 pm 29/11/17

   Copy No.
   1 Section Officer
   2   "   "
   3   "   "
   4
   5 War Diary
   6 File
   7 Brigade
   8 War Diary

                                        H Hecht
                                        for

Army Form C. 2118.

WAR DIARY
INTELLIGENCE SUMMARY.
4TH BN NORTH STAFFORD REGIMENT VOLUME I

(Erase heading not required.)

Instructions regarding War Diaries and Intelligence Summaries are contained in F.S. Regs., Part II. and the Staff Manual respectively. Title pages will be prepared in manuscript. 1ST DECR. — 31ST DECR.

1917

Vol 3

Hour, Date, Place	Summary of Events and Information	Remarks and references to Appendices
1st Decr.	Battalion in the line with headquarters at NORFOLK HOUSE. I.C.N. killed H.O.R. Wounded 2 prisoners captured	
2nd Decr	10.O.R. killed H.O.R. wounded Relieved by 18th Batt. Lancashire Fusiliers. Returned to rest and training at D'Camp.	
4th Decr.	Distribution of ribbons by Lieut. General Sir Claud Jacob K.C.B. to Officers, N.C.O.s and men of the 35th Division.	
5th Decr.	Inspection of training by G.O.C. 35th Division.	
6th Decr	Battalion relieves the 23rd Batt. Manchester Regt in the line with headquarters at Alberta House.	

WAR DIARY
or
INTELLIGENCE SUMMARY.
(Erase heading not required.)

Army Form C. 2118.

Hour, Date, Place	Summary of Events and Information	Remarks and references to Appendices
7th Decr.	4 Prisoners captured	
8th Decr	1 Prisoner captured. Relieved by 2/17th London Regt. No casualties during the tour in the line	
9th Decr	Rest and training at "ROUSSOL and CARDEN FARMS.	
11th Decr	Marched to ROAD CAMP for rest and training	
13th Decr	Inspection of camp by G.O.C. 35th Division	
14 - 31st Decr	Training. Brigade Sports. No 13496 Sjt. G. Moore was awarded the Military medal by the Corps Commander Lieut General Sir Claud Jacob K.C.B on 21st Decr for "gallantry and devotion to duty in the field".	

Sidney Spencer CAPTAIN & ADJT.
5th Bn. NORTH STAFFORDSHIRE REGIMENT.
31/12/17.

WAR DIARY
or
INTELLIGENCE SUMMARY.
(Erase heading not required.)

4th BN NORTH STAFFORD REGIMENT

Instructions regarding War Diaries and Intelligence Summaries are contained in F.S. Regs., Part II. and the Staff Manual respectively. Title pages will be prepared in manuscript.

Remarks and references to Appendices

Vol 4

Hour, Date, Place	Summary of Events and Information	
1st January 1918	Training at ROAD CAMP	
2nd Jan. 1918	— ditto —	
3rd Jan. 1918	Divisional Assault at Arms. Battalion won prize for Marching Steady Complete.	
4th Jan. 1918	Divisional Assault at Arms.	
5th, 6th, 7th Jan 1918.	Training.	
8th Jan. 1918.	Move to front area in relief of 58th Division. Battalion relieved 2/5th London Regt at HUDDLESTONE CAMP.	
9th Jan 1918.	HUDDLESTONE CAMP.	
10th Jan. 1918.	2 O.R. accidentally wounded.	
11th, 12th, 13th, 14th, 15th Jan/18.	Mortar Party.	
16th Jan. 1918.	Relieved Gloucesters Regt on Cross Bank.	
17th Jan. 1918.	2 U.S.A. Officers (Ant. Gas Officers) attached. Mortar Party.	
18th Jan. 1918.	Relieved 11th Bn Sussex Regt at HILLTOP FARM.	
21st Jan. 1918.	Relieved 19th Bn. D.L.I. in Right outsector. Headquarters KRONPRINTZ	
25/26 Jan. 1918.	Two Companies in front line. 1 Support. 1 Reserve. 2 Prisoners taken by "B" Coy.	

WAR DIARY
or
INTELLIGENCE SUMMARY. 4TH BN NORTH STAFFORD REGIMENT.
(Erase heading not required.)

Army Form C

Instructions regarding War Diaries and Intelligence Summaries are contained in F. S. Regs., Part II. and the Staff Manual respectively. Title pages will be prepared in manuscript.

Hour, Date, Place	Summary of Events and Information	Remarks and references to Appendices
27/28 Jan. 1918	Inter Company Relief.	
29 Jan. 1918	Relieved by 4/Worcesters Regt. 88th Brigade, 29° Div. HQ + 1 Coy. move to STEENBECK Strake near HUGEL HALLES. 3 Coys on Corps Line: HUBNER — WORST FARM.	
30 Jan. 1918.	S. O. R. surrender at CORNER COL.	

J.D. Henstock
LIEUT. & A/ADJT.
4 BN. NORTH STAFFORDSHIRE REGIMENT

105th Inf.Bde.
35th Div.

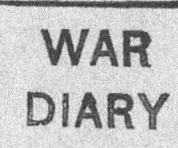

4th BATTN. THE NORTH STAFFORDSHIRE REGIMENT.

February & MARCH

1918

Army Form C. 2118.

WAR DIARY
of
✗✗✗✗✗✗ PARK. 4TH BN NORTH STAFFORD REGIMENT.

Instructions regarding War Diaries and Intelligence Summaries are contained in F.S. Regs., Part II. and the Staff Manual respectively. Title pages will be prepared in manuscript.

Erase heading not required.

Place	Date	Hour	Summary of Events and Information	Remarks and references to Appendices
In the Field	February	1916		
	1.2		In Divisional Support at HILLTOP FARM.	
	3		Moved from HILLTOP FARM to KEMPTON PARK, on transfer from 106th Infy Bde to 108th Infy Bde, in relief of 16th Cheshire Regt. Two companies at KEMPTON PARK & two companies at PHEASANT TRENCH.	
	4		Staff Company relieved KEMPTON PARK & PHEASANT TRENCH.	
	5		Relieved 15th Cheshire Regt in right battalion front. H.Q. – NORFOLK HOUSE. Three companies in line & one in support at PHEASANT TRENCH.	
	6.7.		On right battalion front. Patrols out and along SPREE ROAD, and towards PAPA FARM, and towards SPREE CROSS ROADS. 1 or. killed. 2 or. wounded.	
	8.		Relieved by 2nd K.R.R.C., 1st Division. After relief battalion occupy LARREY CAMP near ELVERDINGHE.	
	9.10.		LARREY CAMP.	
	11.		Moving party as Army Line. Train for ELVERDINGHE – KEMPTON PARK. Move to HUDDLESTONE CAMP in Divisional Support.	
	12.13.14.15.16.		Battalion Working parties on Corps & Army Lines & salvage parties.	
	16		Move to LARREY CAMP in Divisional Reserve.	
	17		Battalion by train to KEMPTON PARK for working parties, digging on Army Line.	
	18		LARREY CAMP. Training & refitting.	
	19		Inspection by G.O.C. 108th Infy Bde, and Brigade Transport Competition	

Army Form C. 2118.

WAR DIARY
INTELLIGENCE 4th Bn NORTH STAFFORD REGIMENT.

Place	Date	Hour	Summary of Events and Information	Remarks and references to Appendices
Inflijite	1918			
Johnson	20.21.		LARREY CAMP. Training.	
	22		Relieved 12th H.L.I. in Brigade Support.	
	23.		Brigade Support.	
	24.		Relieved 13th Gordons Highs in Left Battalion front. H.Q. - PASCAL FARM. 1 O.R. killed. 5 O.R. wounded. Two companies in front line. One Company support. One Company reserve.	
			Details at WELLINGTON CAMP. 1 Officer was O.R. arrived from Division Depot.	
	25		On Left Battalion front. School of 1 Officer & 10 O.R. to TURENNE CROSSING. 2 O.R. killed 5 O.R. wounded	
	26.27.		On Left Battalion front. 1 O.R. killed. 2 O.R. wounded.	
	28			

J.D. Henderson
LIEUT. & ADJT.
4th Bn. NORTH STAFFORDSHIRE REGIMENT.

Army Form C. 2118.

4th North Staffordshire Regt. 105-/35-
35
March. 1918.

JBC 6

WAR DIARY
or
INTELLIGENCE SUMMARY.
(Erase heading not required.)

Instructions regarding War Diaries and Intelligence Summaries are contained in F. S. Regs., Part II. and the Staff Manual respectively. Title Pages will be prepared in manuscript.

Place	Date	Hour	Summary of Events and Information	Remarks and references to Appendices
CANAL BANK NORTH.	1/3/18		Battalion in the line was relieved by 18% Durham Light I. Battalion, on completion of relief, moved to billets at CANAL BANK NORTH, where Details joined the Btn.	
	3/3/18 to 8/3/18		Battalion furnished working parties to work on the Army Line from WELLINGTON CAMP.	
	8/3/18 to 11/3/18		Btn. sent one platoon team per diem to MILLAM to take part in the Divisional Competition for Shooting for prizes given by the Amateur Rifle Association.	
	10/3/18	10.0.A.M	Btn. entrained at BOESINGHE at 10.0. A.M. and proceeded by train to INTERNATIONAL CORNER, & then by route march to ZUIDHUIS CAMP near EIKHOEK. Btn. Transport proceeded to ZUIDHUIS CAMP by road. Btn. became G.H.Q. RESERVE.	
ZUIDHUIS CAMP.	11/3/18 to 22/3/18		Btn. carried out general training. Special training for Bde. and Divisional Competitions at ZUIDHUIS CAMP.	
	12/3/18		Inspector of Catering for 4th Army inspected the cooking arrangements of the Btn. and gave a very favourable report.	
	17/3/18	10.0.A.M	General Plumer, Commanding 4/5 Army, presented ribbons to N.C.O.s and men of the Btn. who had been given rewards for good work in the raid on Feb 28%, at CHAUNY CAMP.	
	18/3/18	2.30 p.m	Btn. wins the Bde. Guard Mounting Competition. Lt. C. S. Dyer O/C Guard. Draft of 29 Other Ranks arrives from Div. Depôt Btn. Btn. wins the Bde. Stretcher Bearers Competition at CHAUNY CAMP. Pte. Briggs wins the Bde. Heavy Weight Boxing Competition.	
	20/3/18		9/Co Company Rapid Firing Competition won by letter "C" Coy.	
	21/3/18		Btn. receives instructions to be ready to move at 12 hours notice. Notification is received that ZERO hour for the move of the Bde. Group will be 4.0. A.M. March 22nd 1918.	

WAR DIARY
INTELLIGENCE SUMMARY
(Erase heading not required.)

Army Form C. 2118.

4⁹ North Staffordshire Regt.

March 1918

Place	Date	Hour	Summary of Events and Information	Remarks and references to Appendices
ZUIDHOUS CAMP.	23/3/18.	1.0 p.m. 2.30 p.m. 4.0 p.m.	Letter "D" Coy. and one Travelling Kitchen proceeded by route march to ROUSBRUGGE Station. Transport moved off at 2.30 p.m. by same route. Btn. less D Coy. and one Travelling Kitchen proceeded by route march to ROUSBRUGGE Station.	
MERICOURT L'ABBE.	24/3/18	8.0 p.m. 9.0 p.m. 11.0 A.M. 12.0 & Noon. 3.15 p.m.	"D" Coy & one Travelling Kitchen left ROUSBRUGGE by train. Btn. & Transport, less D Coy & one Travelling Kitchen left ROUSBRUGGE by train. "D" Coy. and one Travelling Kitchen detrained at MERICOURT L'ABBE. Btn. – Transport, less D Coy. & one Travelling Kitchen, detrained at MERICOURT L'ABBE. Btn. & Transport proceeded by route march to X roads 1½ miles SOUTH of MERICOURT L'ABBE. Where Btn. embussed. All stores, surplus kit &c were dumped at MERICOURT L'ABBE. Btn. debussed at a point 100 WEST of BRAY on the BRAY-CORBIE road. Btn. proceeded by route march to X roads at MARICOURT. Transport proceeded by road from MERICOURT L'ABBE to MARICOURT. Orders were received from 165ᵗʰ INF. BDE. to send two Companies to reinforce the Sherwood Foresters. The remaining two Companies were in Reserve at MARICOURT.	
MARICOURT.	25/3/18	8.50 a.m. 12. Noon. 11. P.M.	After a heavy attack by the enemy the two Companies in Reserve were organised and in conjunction with other troops delivered a counter-attack and restored the line. Casualties:- 1 Off. 8.O.R. Killed. 2 Off. 34.O.R. Wounded. 25.O.R. Missing. The Btn. was relieved by the Lancashire Fusiliers.	
	26/3/18	12.5 A.M. 3.0 A.M.	Orders were received from 165. INF. BDE. to withdraw to the line at BRAY. This was done by 3.30 A.M. The Btn. formed an outpost line on ridge EAST of the BRAY-ALBERT road. This was held until 4 p.m. when orders were received to withdraw to the line BUIRE-DERNANCOURT	

3.   1/4 North Staffordshire Regt.

Army Form C.2118.

WAR DIARY
or
INTELLIGENCE SUMMARY
(Erase heading not required.)

March 1918.

Place	Date	Hour	Summary of Events and Information	Remarks and references to Appendices
BUIRE.	26/3/18	6.15 p.m.	Orders were received to attack and regain the high ground EAST of MORLANCOURT. The Bn. crossed the river ANCRE at DERNAHCOURT and took up a position on the bank running through E.27.d. and K.3.a. Youth could not be gained with the flanks and the Bn. remained in position until ordered to withdraw to the railway line E.19.d.0.0 to CEMETERY. E.20.a.8.3. Casualties:- 1 OFF. 6.O.R. Killed. 51.O.R. Wounded. 1 OFF. 26.O.R. Missing.	
	27/3/18		Held line as above. Relieved at 5 p.m. by Highland Light Infantry Bn. Moved into Support position in Sunken road D.18.d. Casualties:- 3.O.R. Killed. 1 OFF. 22.O.R. Wounded. 12.O.R. Missing.	
	28/3/18	8.0 p.m.	Bn. relieved in a Battalion of 106th INF. BDE. without incident.	
	29/3/18		A raiding party consisting of Lt. Dodman & Lt. Matthews & 25 other ranks endeavoured to dislodge a number of the enemy, who were known to be close to our lines on the opposite banks of the river. The river was successfully crossed, but heavy hostile fire was encountered on the opposite banks. Many casualties were inflicted, and the party withdrew still under fire. Casualties. 2 Other Ranks Killed. 1 OFF. 8.O.R. Wounded.	
	30/3/18		Remained in the line until the night of 30/31 when the Bn. was relieved by a Bn. of the 3rd Australian Division.	
	31/3/18	7.30 A.M.	Bn. moved into Billets at LAHOUSSOYE & immediately started to refit and reorganise.	

April 3rd 1918.

H.L. Hamill Lt. Ast. Adjt.
1/4 North Staffordshire Regt.

Army Form C. 2118.

WAR DIARY
INTELLIGENCE SUMMARY 7th North Staff Regt
(Erase heading not required.)

Vol 7

Place	Date	Hour	Summary of Events and Information	Remarks and references to Appendices
LA HOUSSOYE	1st April		Rest and training (in support to 3rd Div Lusitanians)	
	2nd "		" " "	
	3rd "		" " "	
	4th "		Marched to LA NEUVILLE	
	5th "		at LA NEUVILLE	
	6th "		Marched to TOUTENCOURT	
	7th "		" " HEDAUVILLE	
	8th "		Battalion in line at BOUZINCOURT	
	9th "		1 Officer (Capt R Jordan RAMC killed) 10 O.R killed 2 wounded	
	10th "		30 killed 14 wounded	
	11th "		2 O.R. wounded	
	14th "		Battalion relieved by (106th Bde) ROYAL SCOTS	
	15th "		Billets at HEDAUVILLE	
			6 killed and 24 other ranks wounded	
	16th "		1 officer wounded (Capt F. BACHE) 13 wounded	

WAR DIARY
INTELLIGENCE SUMMARY
4th North Staffs Regt

Army Form C. 2118.

Place	Date	Hour	Summary of Events and Information	Remarks and references to Appendices
	14th Apr		Battalion in line relieves (19th D.L.I.) 104th Inf. Bde.	
	15th Apr		4 O.R. wounded	
	19th Apr		Nil	
	20th Apr		1 O.R. killed 1 O.R. wounded	
	21st Apr		3 O.R. wounded	
	22 Apr		Brigade (104) attacked (Battalion in reserve)	
	23 Apr		Battalion relieves by 18th H.L.I.	
			5 O.R. wounded	
	24th Apr		in support at V.S.a.4.0 - V.S.a.4.9 sheet 57.D.8E.	
	25 Apr		" "	No cas.
	26 Apr		Battalion in line at BOUZINCOURT relieves 17th L.F.s (104 I.B)	
	27		1 killed 2 O.R. wounded	
	28		3 O.R. wounded	
			Nil	
	29		1 O.R. killed	
	30th		Nil	

Jepson Capt & Adjt
4th North Staffs Regt

Army Form C. 2118.

WAR DIARY
or
INTELLIGENCE SUMMARY.
(Erase heading not required.)

4th North Staffordshire Regiment

May 1918

Place	Date	Hour	Summary of Events and Information	Remarks and references to Appendices
BOUZINCOURT	May 1st		Bn in line. Relieved by 10th South Wales Borderers on night 1st/2nd.	
	2		Bn marched by stages to HERISSART, where they were joined by Details & Transport.	
HERISSART	3		from HARPONVILLE.	
	4		Bn in billets & under canvas. Refitting & reorganization commenced.	
	4 to 15		Staff of 4 M.G. & 17 O.R. joined from 3rd Bn North Staffordshire Regt.	
			Special training carried out. — Musketry Competitions.	
	8		Inspection of Bn. by G.O.C. V Corps, presentation of medal ribands.	
	11		Companies inspected at Musketry by the Army Commander Gen. Hon. Sir J.H.G. BYNG, K.C.B., K.C.M.G., M.V.O.	
	15		Bn. moved by march to bank near HEDAUVILLE — WARLOY road, V.8.b. sheet 57 d.	
Bank V.8.c	16 to 19		Working Parties.	
	17		Draft of 65 O.R. joined Bn.	
	20		Bn relieved 2nd Welch Fusiliers in the line at BOUZINCOURT on night 20/21. Capt & Adjt S. JEPSON, Lieut J. CHARLES, 2Lieut J. SPILSBURY.	
Line			Heavy gas shelling by enemy. "gas" and 85 O.R. wounded —	
	23		1 O.R. killed & 6 O.R. wounded.	

WAR DIARY
INTELLIGENCE SUMMARY.

Army Form C. 2118.

4th North Staffordshire Regiment

May 1918

Place	Date	Hour	Summary of Events and Information	Remarks and references to Appendices
	May			
Line BOUZINCOURT	23		Minor raid carried out by Lieut A. STOKA & 27 OR.	
	24		Baths relieved by the 15th Sherwood Foresters	
	25		In Brigade Reserve at BOUZINCOURT	
	26		— do —	
	27		Baths relieve the 15th Cheshire Regt in the Right S. Sector.	
	28		In the line at BOUZINCOURT 1 O.R. killed.	
	29		Draft of 14 Signallers joined Battalion at Transport lines HARPONVILLE	
	30		Draft of 11 OR. joined from 2/6th North Stafford Regt.	
	28	1431	Battn in the line at BOUZINCOURT in Right S. Sector.	

May 31st 1918.

W Newstock? Lieut
4th North Staffordshire Regt.

WAR DIARY or INTELLIGENCE SUMMARY

Army Form C. 2118.

4th North Stafford Regt
June 1918.

Place	Date	Hour	Summary of Events and Information	Remarks and references to Appendices
BOUZINCOURT	June 1st		The Battalion in line in Right Sub Sector relieved by 1st SHERWOOD FORESTERS & became battalion in Reserve. without incident	
	2nd		to B Coys to position W.7.b., A Coy - Trenches W.13.b. C Coy W.13.c.	
	3rd		Draft of 64 O.R joined details at Hedauville	
	4th		B. Coy. 1 O.R. Killed, 4 O.R. wounded.	
HEDAUVILLE	5th		The Battalion was relieved by the 17th LANCASHIRE FUSILIERS & went joined by details at P.33.b.9.8	
			Draft of 51 O.R. from 5th N.STAFFS. 1 O.R. wounded	
	6th		Refitting & Re organisation	
	7th		Training under Coy arrangements. attack formations	
	8th		Battalion practise in attack formation in conjunction with the 15th SHERWOOD FORESTERS in preparation for an offensive on the Right Battalion Sector.	
	9th		Batn relieved 2 coys of the 19th DURHAM L.I. in the right battalion section of the BOUZINCOURT Sector. 1 O.R. wounded.	
	10th			

WAR DIARY
or
INTELLIGENCE SUMMARY.

Army Form C. 2118.

4th N. Staffs.
June 1916.

Place	Date	Hour	Summary of Events and Information	Remarks and references to Appendices
BEUZINCOURT	June 11		A fighting patrol 1 Officer 24 OR got in touch with the enemy inflicted a few casualties. 2/L H.G. KING wounded (since died) 3 OR wounded	
	12		Batt relieved by 19th D.L.I. without incident, moved to R.33.b.9.8.	
MEAULTE	13		Training - Batt. Draft 36 OR from 6th N. Staffs	
	14,15		Lewis Gun training - gas apparatus tested	
	16		Battalion relieved by 11th Cambridgeshire Regt 35th INF. BDE. moved by march route to BEAUQUESNE & billets	
BEAUQUESNE	17		Regt 30% Range made at H.26.b. (map ref 1st Edition Sheet 57A German)	
	18		Training - use of range	
	19		" "	
	20		Route march to Corps winding up by Tactical Scheme	
	21		Artillery formations. Return in attack musketry N.15.b H.26.b. Lt Col D.A.B. Hall rejoins the battalion	
	22		Training - Range work, draft of 2 Off. 4 OR	

WAR DIARY
or
INTELLIGENCE SUMMARY.
(Erase heading not required.)

Army Form C. 2118.

Place	Date	Hour	Summary of Events and Information	Remarks and references to Appendices
BEAUQUESNE	23		Shooting Competition. The line reconnoitred in the ENGLEBELMER Sector	
PUCHEVILLERS	24		The Battalion moved to PUCHEVILLERS by march route & occupied the prisoners cage hutments. (b) attack practice was	
	25		9 200x range – N.26.d. Constructed 30x range. N.27.D	
	26		Training, firing 30x & 200x range. B'de Transport inspected by Major Gen A H MARINDIN DSO A H MARINDIN inspected Transport & officers commented on the turn out. (2/Lt. W.9. Hollingworth)	
	27		Training Coy & Platoon attacks	
	28		Brigade Tactical Scheme	
	29		Divisional musketry meeting	
CANDAS.	30		Batt: moved by march route to CANDAS & there entrained for WIZERNES	

4th North Stafford Regt.   July, 1918.

Army Form C. 2118.

Vol 10

WAR DIARY
or
INTELLIGENCE SUMMARY.
(Erase heading not required.)

Instructions regarding War Diaries and Intelligence Summaries are contained in F. S. Regs., Part II. and the Staff Manual respectively. Title pages will be prepared in manuscript.

Place	Date	Hour	Summary of Events and Information	Remarks and references to Appendices
WIZERNES	July. 1st	7.0 AM	"B" Coy and Cooker detained on arrival from CANDAS.	
		9.0 AM	Btn. (less "B" Coy. & Cooker) detained on arrival from CANDAS.	
		12 NOON	Btn. proceeded by route march to MORINGHEM and PETIT DIEQUES, arriving at	
		3.30 p.m.	B.H.Q. and "B" Coy. billeted at MORINGHEM with Transport. "A" "C" and "D"	
			Coys. billeted at PETIT DIEQUES. Btn. in XIX 5 Corps.	
	2nd	12.NOON.	Transport moved by Route march to ARQUES.	
	3rd	5. A.M.	Transport moved by Route march to Aerodrome ABEELE arriving 4 p.m.	
		8. A.M.	Btn. (less Transport) moved by Motor Bus to Aerodrome ABEELE arriving 2.30 p.m.	
	4th	9. P.M.	Btn. relieved Support Btn. of 358th French Regt. at MONT ROUGE.	
MONT ROUGE	5-8		Btn. dug in, wired, and wired into system of trenches on MONT ROUGE	
	9th	10. P.M.	Btn. relieved 15th Cheshire Regt. in the front System, disposition C. D & A Coys	
			in front line "C" & "D", "B" Coy in reserve without incident.	
	7th		1 O.R. Killed 1 O.R. wounded	
	6th		Capt D.C.B.COTES, Lt D F HOLMES, Lt W.G.H. COOPER-KING joined the battalion at Details.	
	11th		Reinforcement 21 O.R. 1 O.R. Killed 3 O.R. wounded	
	13		1. O.R. died	

(A7883) D, D, & L., London, E.C. Wt. W869/M1652 350/000 4/17 Forms/C/2118/14

Army Form C. 2118.

WAR DIARY
or
INTELLIGENCE SUMMARY.
(Erase heading not required.)

Instructions regarding War Diaries and Intelligence Summaries are contained in F. S. Regs., Part II. and the Staff Manual respectively. Title pages will be prepared in manuscript.

Place	Date	Hour	Summary of Events and Information	Remarks and references to Appendices
	13	11 P.M.	Bt. relieved by 15th Sherwood Foresters without incident & proceeded to Reserve Position in Billets at ROYKENS AKKER – were joined by advance from R.H.Q. 0.5 (Sheet 27)	
	14		Regimental Band Reformed (1st time since arrival of Bn. in France.	
			Baths by Coys at GODEWAERAVELDE	
	17	9 am	Bn. proceeded by route march to relieve the 15th CHESHIRE REGT in the intermediate system at MONT ROUGE	
			Sgt J BRANDON awarded the Meritorious Service Medal	
	20		Qmr. Hon/Lt A. HODGSON & 8 O.R. joined the Batt at Details	
			P.M.C & P.R.I a/15 inst.	
	21		Bn relieve 15/Cheshire Regt in the Front line near LOCRE	
	28		2/Lt T.H.Paulton carried out a raid on enemy post with one Platoon. Zero 1:55 am	

WAR DIARY or INTELLIGENCE SUMMARY

Army Form C. 2118.

Instructions regarding War Diaries and Intelligence Summaries are contained in F. S. Regs., Part II. and the Staff Manual respectively. Title pages will be prepared in manuscript.

(Erase heading not required.)

Place	Date	Hour	Summary of Events and Information	Remarks and references to Appendices
	23rd		The patrols found to be unoccupied. No casualties to the party.	
	25th		Btn relieved in the line by 15/S Kennings. Marched to Reserve to Reserve Billets near BOISEHOEPE. Weather cold & wet.	
			Total casualties for the eight days O.R. 4 killed 13 wounded.	
	27th		Officers Mess Meeting – the first in this country. Capt G.B. elected President. Capt. WORSLEY M.G & Lieuts NORMAN 2/R BARRETT as members.	
	29th		Btn relieves 15/Cheshire Regt in the support position (LOURE) without incident.	
	30		20 O.R. Reinforcements arrived also in Rest Camp chiefly 2/6 Bn[?] Lt Hughs R.A.M.C. Regimental M.O. assumes (C. of Duty). Reports from Capt. Johnson Rest Camp that fellow has won a Silver cup for bullet & bayonet competition and congratulation by Corps and Divisional Commanders on the Lewis gun team in the competition.	
	31st			

H. Meredith Capt.
for O.C.

4TH BN. NORTH STAFFORD REGT. **WAR DIARY** or **INTELLIGENCE SUMMARY**.

AUGUST 1918. Army Form C. 2118.

SHEET 95

Place	Date	Hour	Summary of Events and Information	Remarks and references to Appendices
In the field	Aug. 1st	1.0 AM	Bn. relieved the 15th Cheshire Regt. in the front line position of the centre subsector in the LOCRE Sector. Relief complete by 10.0 a.m. Reinforcements 40 O.R. joined the Bn. at the Details Camp.	
	2nd		Lt. B.F.S. POTTER evacuated to F.A. Sick. 42772. Pte. W. Laverick. C. Coy and 46583 Pte. E.W. Hutes. C. Coy awarded the Military Medal for gallantry and devotion to duty in action on July 24th 1918.	
	3rd		Reinforcements 4 O.R. joined the Bn. at Details Camp. Casualty. One O.R. Wounded. Inter Company Relief. B Coy relieved A Coy in the Left Front Position. C Coy relieved D. Coy in the Right Front Position.	
	4th		Casualty. One O.R. Wounded.	
	5th		Casualty. One O.R. Wounded. Bn. relieved by the 15th Cheshire Regt. in the front line position. Relief complete at 11.45 p.m. On relief Bn. moved to Reserve Positions at Camp near BOESCHEPE.	
	6th		Bn. rested and bathed at camp near BOESCHEPE.	

Army Form C. 2118.

SHEET 2

4TH BN. NORTH STAFFORD REGT. WAR DIARY AUGUST. 1918.
or
INTELLIGENCE SUMMARY.
(Erase heading not required.)

Place	Date	Hour	Summary of Events and Information	Remarks and references to Appendices
BOESCHEPE	7th		Casualty. One O.R. wounded.	
	8th		Btn. relieved in the Reserve Position by 2/14th London Regt. 90th Brigade, 30th Division. 35th Division came into Corps Reserve. On relief Btn. moved to billets and camps near ST. SILVESTRE CAPPEL. Band & Coys. B.H.Q. arrived in new camp at 8.30.p.m.	
near ST. SILVESTRE CAPPEL.	9th		A and D Coys. arrived in new camp at 3.45.A.M.	
	10th		Btn. rested. General clean up.	
	11th	10.AM	Capt. S.J. Worsley. M.C., 4868. C.S.M. E. Dale D.C.M., 49272. Sgt. W. Johnson D.C.M. 37621. Cpl. S.J. Townend. M.M., 46636. Pte. A. Askwey M.M. represented the Btn. at a Special Parade Service before His Majesty the King at TERDEGHEM.	
	12.		Training Carried out.	
	13.		Training Carried out. 9th Company Football Matches.	
	14.		23391. L/Sgt. W. HEATHCOTE awarded the Military Medal for gallantry and devotion to duty in action on July 30/31 1918 Capt. (A/Major) N.G. P. de C. TRONSON and 2/Lt. S. GOODYEAR joined the Btn. for duty. Training carried out. Inter Company football matches.	

4TH BN. NORTH STAFFORD REGT. WAR DIARY AUGUST, 1918. Army Form C. 2118.
or
INTELLIGENCE SUMMARY. SHEET. III

Place	Date	Hour	Summary of Events and Information	Remarks and references to Appendices
ST. SYLVESTRE CAPPEL. In the field	Aug. 15		Training carried out. 2/Lt. B.C. WHISTLER joined for duty, having received a direct commission on the field. Inter Company football matches.	
	16th		Training carried out. 9th Coy. Company football matches.	
			2/Lt. A.L. JOHNSON joined the Btn. for duty	
	17th		Training carried out. Football match Officers v. Sergeants. Sergeants won. 3-1.	
	19th		Training carried out.	
	20th		Training carried out. Major H. Meredith assumed temporary command of the Battalion on Lt. Col. D.M.B. Hall proceeding on leave to U.K. 2/Lt. [?] or joined 19th or S/bn Bn. as reinforcements.	
	21st		Training carried out. "A" Coy. won the inter Company football Competition, to decide which Coy. should represent the Btn.	
	22nd		Training carried out. Inter Company football matches	
	23rd		"A" Coy beaten by "X" Company of 153rd Cheshire Regt. in Bde. football Competition.	
	24th		Training carried out. Inter Company football matches.	
	25th		Officers new hockey XI. Sports Committee formed consisting of Capt. D.C.B. COTES.	

WAR DIARY
or
INTELLIGENCE SUMMARY.
(Erase heading not required.)

4TH BN. NORTH STAFFORD REGT.   AUGUST. 1918.   Army Form C. 2118.
                                                              SHEET. 4.

Place	Date	Hour	Summary of Events and Information	Remarks and references to Appendices
ST. SILVESTRE CAPPEL.	Aug. 25th		2/Lt. H.D. BRAND, 2/Lt. S. GOODYER and 2/Lt. T.H. PRESTON.	
	26th		Training carried out.	
	27.		Inter Coy. Competitions — Bayonet Fighting — Physical Training — Guard Drill — Firing on the Miniature Range — won by No 16 Platoon. D. Coy.	
	28.		Inter Coy. Football match won by "B" Coy.	
	29. 30.		The Bn. moved by Light Railway to BOESCHEPE and relieved the 12th Royal Irish Rifles in the Support Position (Brigade in Support) in the ST. JANS CAPPEL Sector. Relief complete by 9.15. p.m. Aug. 29th.	
BOESCHEPE.	30. 31.		The Bn. was relieved in the Support Position – ST. JANS CAPPEL Sector – by 12th Royal Irish Rifles.(363 Div.) Relief complete by 12.15 A.M. Aug. 31. Bn. travelled by light Railway to billets near ST. SILVESTRE CAPPEL, arriving at 4. A.M. Aug. 31st.	

W. Hamill Capt. Adjt
4th North Staffds. Regt.

WAR DIARY or INTELLIGENCE SUMMARY.

(Erase heading not required.)

Army Form C. 2118.

4th North Staffordshire Regiment

Vol 72

Place	Date 1916 Sep	Hour	Summary of Events and Information	Remarks and references to Appendices
ST SYLVESTRE CAPPEL	1		Training.	
	2		Proceeded by march route to TUNNELLING CAMP PROVEN no number out on the line of march.	
	4		The Batt. entrained proceeded to 'ALE SIDING hence by march route relieved the 3/120 Regt. U.S.A. in the LEFT SUB-SECTOR, CANAL SECTOR at Spoil Bank without incident. D Coy Line, A Coy Support B. C. Reserve. B Coy heavily gassed 17 O.R. Gassed	
	6		5 O.R. Wounded. Active patrolling by day, night was successfully carried out during the tour	
	7		3 O.R. Wounded, 1 O.R. Killed	
	8		The Batt. was relieved by the 18 Lanc. Fusiliers & proceeded to Billets Reserve B.H.Q. ERIE CAMP (the same as occupied by the Bn. Jan 5th 1916.) B Coy at YKAMERTINGHE MILL, A.B.C. Coys BRANDHOEK 1 O.R. Wounded	
	9		Batt registering & improving Killeen Sd Road.	
	12		1 O.R. Killed 4 O.R. Wounded	

WAR DIARY
or
INTELLIGENCE SUMMARY.
(Erase heading not required.)

Army Form C. 2118.

Place	Date	Hour	Summary of Events and Information	Remarks and references to Appendices
	Sep 12		The Batt relieved the 12th H.L.I the Right Sub-Sector CANAL SECTOR. The casualties were questioned during relief. Considerable shelling & was thought that the enemy anticipated the relief taking place.	
	14		Patrols reconnoitred our FRENCH TRENCH BUS HOUSE	
	15		35th Div with 104. Inf Bde on left, 105 Inf Bde on Right advanced to line at an average distance of 500x. % D"s Ia issued by posts herein mentioned were occupied without resistance. 1 OR wounded. % N° 42 moved to N° more of the 16th	
	16		2/Lt P.N. SHELLEY & 6 OR reconnoitred St ELOI CRATERS. The Battn was relieved by the 15th Cheshire Regt without incident & proceeded to billets - H.22.a. 5 OR Reinforcements	
	18		A Raid on ST ELOI CRATERS being ordered to be executed by 4 platoons of B Coy was cancelled at the last moment. 2/Lt S. WILLIAMS & 2/Lt H. H. PICKFORD were posted to the Batt.	

WARDIARY
or
INTELLIGENCE SUMMARY.
(Erase heading not required.)

Army Form C. 2118.

Place	Date	Hour	Summary of Events and Information	Remarks and references to Appendices
	Sep 19		The Battalion proceeded to SCHOOL CAMP. They entrained at YALE SIDING, detrained at BLUE GRASS Range (by march route	
	20		Rev. S. D. Blackman Cr attached	
	21		Batts. rect. 2c Sparkets 33rd Div. Cmced Party Marked to Camp	
	22		The Battalion moved forward by Bus & march route to occupy position. Reviously Reconnoitred from the 18th Hill. Battalion HQdS BEDFORD HOUSE. Lt Col DMB HALL reposoned Im. Monkled R.	
	23		The Battalion was relieved by 2 coys of 15th CHESHIRE entrained & proceeded to SCHOOL CAMP	
	24		2/Lts A.LBRAIN BCWOOD FCBOWLES JDUTTON Joined the Battalion from Div Recephn Camp. Count VON CALON, BELGIAN INTERPRETER attached 2 ORs Wounded.	

WAR DIARY
or
INTELLIGENCE SUMMARY.
(Erase heading not required.)

Army Form C. 2118.

Place	Date	Hour	Summary of Events and Information	Remarks and references to Appendices
	SEP 25		Operation Orders for the 26th issued C47. Coy Commanders inspected a Range Model of Battle Front at CASSEL	
	26		Proceeded by Bus & march route to the Forward area & relieved part of the 15th CHESHIRE REGT. The Battalion Coy Commanders. Capt S.J.WORSLEY YMCA Coy, Lt P.N. NORMAN. B Coy. Capt M.D.GIB. C Coy, Lt H.WOODWARD M.M. D Coy.	
	27.		Reconnoitring Patroles very busy during the early hours with assembly positions which were occupied at night ready for jumping off. 1 OR killed. 2 OR wounded by his own guns.	
	28		The Batt took part in an attack for fertile time since our came to FRANCE. assembly was completed successfully by 0800am. The Objectives of the Batt. TRIANGULAR BLUFF? BUFFS BANK. Zero was at 05.30. By 0800 the Batt had gained all objectives capturing some 300 prisoners	

WAR DIARY
or
INTELLIGENCE SUMMARY.
(Erase heading not required.)

Army Form C. 2118.

Place	Date	Hour	Summary of Events and Information	Remarks and references to Appendices
	29		1 Steel Gun, 1 Heavy & 2 light Trench mortars, 10 Machine Guns. Cavalier Capt M.D.Gib. Capt W.L.HARROD 2Lt H.D.BRAND wounded. 5 O.R. Killed 29 wounded 4 missing. The behaviour of all ranks throughout the battle was magnificent & the battalion was complimented on its work by the Brigade & Divisional Commander. Night spent in consolidating the position. The following Officers took part. In command Lt Col E.M.B. HALL. Adjutant Capt W.L. HARRIS. Intelligence Officer 2Lt H.BARRETT. Signalling Officer 2Lt P.G. CALLADINE. M.O. Lt J.T.HUGHES R.A.M.C. Coy Commanders Capt S.J.WORSLEY M.C. Lt B.C.D.NORMAN. Capt M.D.GIB. Lt H.WOODWARD M.M. Platoon Commanders 2Lt T.H.PRESTON. 2Lt W.G. BARNESS 2Lt B.C. WHISTLER. 2Lt S.F.GOODYER. 2Lt S.WILLIAMS. 2Lt H.H.PICKFORD. Lt HOLMES. 2Lt A.L.JOHNSON. 2Lt R. TURLEY	

WAR DIARY
or
INTELLIGENCE SUMMARY.
(Erase heading not required.)

Army Form C. 2118.

Place	Date	Hour	Summary of Events and Information	Remarks and references to Appendices
	28		2/Lt F.E.CORP. 2/Lt H.D BRAND & Lt J.E HUDSON. Lt C.S DYER appointed acting adjutant. 2/Lt H.BARRETT acting asst adj. 2/Lt OXLOYD intelligence officer.	
	29		At 5.30.am The battalion moved to KLEIN ZILLEBEKE from hence to ZANDVOORDE which latter place was reported to be held by us but was in reality held by the enemy. The Brigade was drawn up outside ZANDVOORDE 1st MG line. The 15th Cheshire Regt attacked unsuccessfully at 12.30 pm. At 3 pm the 4th "Staffs" & "15" Sherwood Foresters attacked ZANDVOORDE RIDGE which carried the Reading Corps to lose direction slightly. This however was at once rectified & the batt advanced under very heavy MG fire & captured ZANDVOORDE. The night was spent consolidating the ground gained on the line ZANDVOORDE - TEN BRIELEN.	

WAR DIARY
or
INTELLIGENCE SUMMARY.

Army Form C. 2118.

Place	Date	Hour	Summary of Events and Information	Remarks and references to Appendices
	29		Casualties were as follows 2/Lt B C WHISTLER killed Lt B C NORMAN - 2Lt I H PRESTON died of wounds OR 17 killed, 143 wounded 24 missing	
	30		At 6.15am The Brigade continued its advance to on WERVICQ Debatt. were in Reserve & did get into action had day + night Spent in TENBRIELEN OR.s 2 killed 1 wounded Reinforcements 11 OR	

B Byay F
O/C 4 Staffs Regt

4th Bn. North Staff

Army Form C. 2118.

WAR DIARY
or
INTELLIGENCE SUMMARY.
(Erase heading not required.)

October 1918

Instructions regarding War Diaries and Intelligence Summaries are contained in F.S. Regs., Part II. and the Staff Manual respectively. Title pages will be prepared in manuscript.

Place	Date 1918 Oct	Hour	Summary of Events and Information	Remarks and references to Appendices
TENBRIELEN	1		In the early hours of the morning the Pill boxes were heavily shelled, one direct hit causing several casualties. At 4 p.m the Battn being relieved by the 6 Cheshire Regt, proceeded to KRUISEECKE where the night was spent. Casualties 2 Killed 5 Wounded	
	2		Shelled out of camp about 9 am so pushed another ½ mile about 500 yds away. Remained undisturbed until night.	
	3		At 3 am the Battn proceeded to Rest Billets at arriving about 7.30 am. Spent the day resting, bivouacs etc.	
	4		General cleaning up. Kit inspections. Battns	
	5		Bathing, improving billets etc. Reinforcements 2 O.R.	
	6		Training, salvage & improving billets	
	7		Company Commanders reconnoitred forward positions Training Bathing	
	8		Practice attack by 2 Companies over battlefield Collecting trophies from field of battle. Reinforcements 1 O.R.	

A6945 Wt. W1422/M1160 350,000 12/16 D. D. & L. Forms/C/2118/14

Army Form C. 2118.

WAR DIARY
or
INTELLIGENCE SUMMARY.
(Erase heading not required.)

Instructions regarding War Diaries and Intelligence Summaries are contained in F. S. Regs., Part II. and the Staff Manual respectively. Title pages will be prepared in manuscript.

Place	Date 1918 Oct.	Hour	Summary of Events and Information	Remarks and references to Appendices
	9		Practice Attack by 2 Companies over Battlefield. Battng & Training	
	10		Coy & Sgn Offrs & Scout Offr reconnoitred forward position having under Coy arrangements.	
	11		The Battn moved to the forward area and took up a position as Reserve at K.21.c. near MOLENHOEK. Reinforcements 1 Officer	
	12		Line was reconnoitred by Company Commanders arrangements completed for the attack. Casualties 1 O.R. wounded.	
	13		Assembly successfully completed by ZERO – 1 hour. At ZERO + 30 Battn which was in Bgde Reserve moved forward.	
	14		The industry was to a large fog but the direction was nevertheless well kept. The Battn passed through the 15 th Cheshire Regt	

A6943 Wt. W14422/M1160 350,000 12/16 D. D. & L. Forms/C./2118/14.

WAR DIARY
or
INTELLIGENCE SUMMARY.
(Erase heading not required.)

Army Form C. 2118.

Place	Date	Hour	Summary of Events and Information	Remarks and references to Appendices
			and reinforced the 15th Sherwood Foresters who were held up in & around KLEEF HOEK. The fog had by now lifted & we were much hampered by enemy M.G. & by a lack of artillery support. Further advance was found to be impossible & the Batt^n dug in my front of KAPPEL HOEK. The following Officers took part in the attack. Captn H. Hosack, Lt M. Preston, 2 Lt M.G. Barnes and 2 Lt J. Dutton. Captn A.L. Thynne, 2 Lt S.B. Burgess 2 Lt H.A. Pickford, 2 Lt L. Williams, Capt D.E.B. Catto 2 Lt R. Turley, 2 Lt K.R. Brown, Captn J.E. De Frayas, 2 Lt F.E. Cosp, 2 Lt F.C. Bowles, 2 Lt G.B. Ellinor, 2 Lt Col. D.B.B. Hall. 13 Sergeant Headquarters Lt Col. B.S. Dyer, 2 Lt O. Lloyd Intelligence Officer, 2 Lt P.G. Galloway Signals Officer	

WAR DIARY or INTELLIGENCE SUMMARY

Army Form C. 2118.

Place	Date	Hour	Summary of Events and Information	Remarks
	15		Casualties killed Capt. & Adjt. Johnson and 5 O.R.s. Died of Wounds Capt. D.E.B. Botha. Wounded Capt. J.F.P. De Trojes, 2 Lt W.G. Burgers and 33 O.R.s, 7 O.R.s Missing. The Battⁿ attacked at 9 a.m. in conjunction with the 10th Brigade & captured & consolidated the high ground S.E. of KAPPELHOEK. There was some sharp fighting, but the opposition was soon broken down & all objectives taken according to plan. The same Officers took part as on previous day. Less casualties. The following casualties were incurred. Wounded 2/Lt T.G. Burgess 2/Lt A.H. Pickford, 2/Lt Dutton, 33 O.R.s (From previous day) 7 O.R.s Killed 4 2 Wounded & missing. Captured on 14th & 15th included 106 Prisoners	

WAR DIARY or INTELLIGENCE SUMMARY

Army Form C. 2118.

Place	Date	Hour	Summary of Events and Information	Remarks and references to Appendices
	16		35 Baching tups H. Field Guns. Batt" moved to west Gulleto as Brigade Reserve at MURRAY HOUSE with B.H.Q. at CLARINETTE FARM. Bn. re-equipped & re-dug.	
	17		2 O.R.s wounded. Baths & change of clothing. Congratulatory message from Bny. Gen. head to all ranks on the results of the recent operations. Reinforcement of 1 Offr Capt J.C. Richards.	
	18		28.45 hours the Batt" moved to assembly positions between LAUWE and MARCKE.	
	19		The assembly was successfully completed by 02.00 hours. 10th Inf. Bgde attacked at 5.30 hours & successfully captured all objectives. Batt" moved with remainder of Bgde into MARCKE. That afternoon the Batt" moved into COURTRAI	

WAR DIARY or INTELLIGENCE SUMMARY

Army Form C. 2118.

Place	Date	Hour	Summary of Events and Information	Remarks and references to Appendices
	20		which was being heavily shelled. 30 casualties. The Batt. remained short for the night. At 04.15 hours the Batt. moved to the Escaille positions between COURTRAI - BLOKKEM while deploying up assembly positions the Batt. was fired on from three sides by M.G.'s in Farm. These however were quickly dealt with & the attack commenced at 05.30 hours with the 15 Sherwood Foresters on Right & 29th Div. on the Left. The attack lasted all day the enemy putting up a very stiff fight, with M.G.'s 4 Field Guns, Trench Mortars, and also two 5.9 Hows firing at point blank range. The objective was finally reached & consolidated about midnight, all ranks of the Batt. displayed the greatest gallantry	

WAR DIARY or INTELLIGENCE SUMMARY

Army Form C. 2118.

(Erase heading not required.)

Instructions regarding War Diaries and Intelligence Summaries are contained in F. S. Regs., Part II. and the Staff Manual respectively. Title pages will be prepared in manuscript.

Place	Date	Hour	Summary of Events and Information	Remarks and references to Appendices
	21		detrognates & engineers and men employed in trenches by both the Brigadier & Lieut General. Captures announced as 37 Prisoners 11 Machine Guns 1 Light Trench Mortar & two 5.9 How. The same Officers took part as on the 15th less casualties. In addition the following Officers took part. Capt. J. G. Richards, Lt. W.H. Bend, Lt. H.P. Boxer, Lt. A. Perrot, 2/Lt. E.G.L. Davies, 2/Lt. E. Eagings, 2/Lt. B. Stozeley. Casualties as follows Wounded Capt. J. G. Richards, A.N. Proctor 2/Lt. B. Stozeley O.Rs 12 killed 73 Wounded 6 missing. The Battn held their objective (SWEVEGHAM.) until the KRRs & 41st Div. passed through them.	
	22		Moved to Billets between SWEVEGHAM — COURTRAI & about mid day marched to COURTRAI & occupied	

WAR DIARY
or
INTELLIGENCE SUMMARY.

(Erase heading not required.)

Army Form C. 2118.

Place	Date	Hour	Summary of Events and Information	Remarks and references to Appendices
			Billets in the Barracks. The Band are engaged	
			Rehearsing. 1 O.R.	
			Under authority delegated by the Field Marshall	
			Commander in Chief the Corps Commander has awarded	
			the following decorations for gallantry & devotion	
			to duty.	
			Bar to Military Medal	
			46096 Sgt J.M. Woodcock E.Coy	
			Military Medal	
			42633 Pte J. Russell	
			42651 " T. South	
			46575 " L. Hall	
			42875 L/pl J. Burrell	
			421,327 Pte A.J. Wilson	
			45,552 " N. Waldon	
			23,386 Sgt E. Guilder	

WAR DIARY
or
INTELLIGENCE SUMMARY.
(Erase heading not required.)

Army Form C. 2118.

Place	Date	Hour	Summary of Events and Information	Remarks and references to Appendices
	23		4.3.6.74. L/cpl J. Derbyshire 4.2.6.23. L/cpl H. Progress 35.795. Pte. W.C. Lawton	
	24		Reorganizing	
	25		Do	
			Do	
	26		The Battn moved to billets near SWEVEGHAM	
	27		Transport joined the Battn. Training. Reinforcements 16 O.R.	
	28		Inspection. Training.	
	29		Training. Reinforcements 1 O.R.	
	30		Training.	
	31		Training. The following awards were made for gallantry & devotion to duty. Distinguished Service Order. Lt. Col. D. J. B. Hall Capt. S. J. Worley D.C.	

WAR DIARY
or
INTELLIGENCE SUMMARY.
(Erase heading not required.)

Army Form C. 2118.

Place	Date	Hour	Summary of Events and Information	Remarks and references to Appendices
			Military Cross	
			Capt. B. D. Gill	
			Lieut H. Woodward D.S.O.	
			2/Lt W.G. Barnes	
			Distinguished Conduct Medal	
			38,531 Pte H. Holt	
			45284 " Cpl. Silbury	
			40911 " L/Cpl Bratton	
			A. Barrett 2/Lt	
			for	
			O/C 1/6th North Staffs Regt	

H⁴ Bn. North Staff

Army Form C. 2118.

WAR DIARY
INTELLIGENCE SUMMARY

NOVEMBER 1918

Place	Date	Hour	Summary of Events and Information	Remarks and references to Appendices
SWEVEGHEM	1		Training was continued during the morning. The Batt⁴ proceeded by route march to Billets in the MARCKE area, starting at 15.10 hours. Reinforcements 1 Officer 2ⁿᵈ M.I. Liney	
MARCKE	2		Training & changing billets.	
	3		The Batt⁴ attended a Brigade Church Parade held in the factory at MARCKE, and afterwards the Div. General had a march past.	
	4		Training and bathing. Reinforcements 1 Off⁴ 2ⁿᵈ E.A. REEVES 43 O.R's	
	5		The Companies Officer recognised forward positions. Training. C & D Companies practised forward bridging.	
	6		Same bge bridging. Training by Coy's in recognised forward area. Reinforcements 2 Officers, Lt J. M. SKEAFF and 2Lt W. G. CLARKE.	
	7		Batt⁴ moved to billets in COURTRAI. Reinforcements 1 O.R.	

Army Form C. 2118.

WAR DIARY
or
INTELLIGENCE SUMMARY.
(Erase heading not required.)

Instructions regarding War Diaries and Intelligence Summaries are contained in F. S. Regs., Part II. and the Staff Manual respectively. Title pages will be prepared in manuscript.

Place	Date	Hour	Summary of Events and Information	Remarks and references to Appendices
COURTRAI	8		Training	
	9		The Battⁿ moved forward to relieve the 15th Sherwoods in the front line, but owing to the enemy retiring, proceeded to INGOYGHEM where the Battⁿ was kept in billets. Reinforcements, CAPT. F.E. WENGER & 2LT W.R. OLLIS	
INGOYGHEM	10		Crossed the river SCHELDT and occupied billets at G 32d and 983 c, near PENSEMONT, remaining there until next day	
PENSEMONT	11		Moved forward again to billets at M 34. a 5.6. Hostilities ceased at 11.00 hours.	
	12		Training. Reinforcements 4 O.R.^s (Signallers)	
	13		Battⁿ moved back to billets at X 3. c 1.2. near	
RENAIX	14		Training	
	15		Training	
	16		Training	

WAR DIARY
INTELLIGENCE SUMMARY.
(Erase heading not required.)

Army Form C. 2118.

Place	Date	Hour	Summary of Events and Information	Remarks and references to Appendices
RENAIX	Nov. 17		The Battn attended Divl Church Parade, which was followed by a presentation of Gen. Ribands by the G.O.C. 35th Div.	
	18		Training	
	19		Companies the moved back to billets in the COURTRAI area. Halted at OKKERWIJK where the night was spent in billets.	
HEULE	20		Proceeded to billets at HEULE near COURTRAI. Reinforcements 2 Officers 2/Lt W.R. BRACEY and 2/Lt J. DUTTON	
	21		Training. Reinforcements 1 Officer, Captn A.G.S.M. BROOKSBANK 2 O.R's.	
	22		Training. Reinforcements	
	23		Training. The following Officers awarded the MILITARY CROSS for gallantry & devotion to duty. Captn H. HENSTOCK, Captn C.S. DYER, Captn D.F. HOLMES, Captn W.H. BIRD, Lt O. LLOYD.	
	24		Battn attended Brigade Church Parade, held in the Square of the township at HEULE.	

Army Form C. 2118.

WAR DIARY
or
INTELLIGENCE SUMMARY.
(Erase heading not required.)

Place	Date	Hour	Summary of Events and Information	Remarks and references to Appendices
HEULE	24		Reinforcements 4 Officers Capt H.E. Fawcett Lt E.V.B. Williams, Capt R.B. Taylor, 2Lt H.F. Evans.	
	25		Batt took part in a Brigade Route March	
	26		Training and Bathing	
	27		Training. Reinforcements 1 Officer 2 Lt L. Pearse and 28 O.Rs	
HEULE	28		Moved by route march to the GHELUWE area where Batt billeted for the night. Route, GULLEGHEM -SCHOONWATER- WEVELGHEM- MENIN - GHELUWE.	
GHELUWE	29		Marched to billets in the POPERINGHE area. Route GHELUWE - GHELUVELT - YPRES - POPERINGHE.	
POPERINGHE	30		Batt continued the march as far as TERDEGHEM where the night was spent in billets. Route POPERINGHE - ABEELE - STEENVOORDE - TERDEGHEM.	

H Barrett 2/Lt
for
O.C. 4th/5th Loyal N. Lanc. Regt.

WAR DIARY
or
INTELLIGENCE SUMMARY.
(Erase heading not required.)

Army Form C. 2118.

4 N Staff

Vol 15

Place	Date	Hour	Summary of Events and Information	Remarks and references to Appendices
	Dec.y			
TERDEGHEM	1		The Batt.n moved by route march to the WULVERDINGHE area. Route STEENVOORDE — CASSEL ROAD — SWITCH once N. of CASSEL along map CASSEL — LEDERZEELE Road — WULVERDINGHE. Remained there in billets for the night.	
WULVERDINGHE	2		Batt.n marched to BAYENGHEM. Route WATTEN — ESTMONT — QUEST MONT — BAYENGHEM. C. arrived &c. Batt.n settled in billets. Reinforcements 1 O.R.	
BAYENGHEM	3		Inspection & cleaning	
	4		Training & cleaning	
	5		Training	
	6		Training	
	7		Training. Batt.n Cross Country Run was held, also Ranks taking part. Reinforcements 1 O.R.	
	8		Church Parade held in an Orchard N. of BAYENGHEM. CHURCH. Bathing. Reinforcements 1 O.R. The award of the CROIX DE GUERRE approved	

Army Form C. 2118.

WAR DIARY
or
INTELLIGENCE SUMMARY.
(Erase heading not required.)

Instructions regarding War Diaries and Intelligence Summaries are contained in F. S. Regs., Part II. and the Staff Manual respectively. Title pages will be prepared in manuscript.

Place	Date	Hour	Summary of Events and Information	Remarks and references to Appendices
BAYENGHEM	Dec 8		by the Insph d'authorities to	
	9		2 Lt. R. TURLEY CROIX DE GUERRE à l'ordre de DIVISION	
			H.1370 PTE W.A. SNELLING Do do BRIGADE	
			The Batt moved to NORTLEULINGHEM where billets were occupied	
NORTLEULINGHEM	10		Sunday. 1 Coy Route Band for remainder of Batt?	
	11		Training. 1 Coy felling up trestles	
	12		Batt firing on Range at P.2.L. postponed owing to the weather	
	13		2 Coy less 1 platoon proceeded to 98a for Salvage work as trenches. Training & Gunnery. Demobilization. 27 O.R.s proceeded to Dispersal Camp	
	14		Training. Demobilization. 26 O.R.s proceeded to Dispersal Camp Parade	
	15		Batt? Church Parade. Reinforcements 1 O.R.	
	16		Batt? proceeded to Range at P.12.L. & fired Practice 2 Demobilization. 26 O.R.s proceeded to Dispersal Camp	

Army Form C. 2118.

WAR DIARY
or
INTELLIGENCE SUMMARY.
(Erase heading not required.)

Instructions regarding War Diaries and Intelligence Summaries are contained in F. S. Regs., Part II. and the Staff Manual respectively. Title pages will be prepared in manuscript.

Place	Date	Hour	Summary of Events and Information	Remarks and references to Appendices
NORTLEOLINGHEM	Dec 17		Clothing Inspection & Musketry Instruction	
	18		20 Grms proceeded to Dispersal Camp. Batteries & Letters or Re-established and Batteries of Service by Lt Col D.M.B. HALL D.S.O.	
	19		Musketry & Training	
	20		Bathing & Musketry. Batt Transport were judged wagons of the Brigade Transport Competition, showing the percentage of 89½ %	
	21		Musketry & Training. Batt Transport obtained 2nd place in the Div. Transport Competition. Demobilization. The first Officer Lt W. COOPER-KING proceeded to Dispersal Camp	
	22		Batt paraded for Divine Service on Batt Parade Ground	
	23		Batt proceeded to Range at P.12.b. to fire repetition of casuals.	

Army Form C. 2118.

WAR DIARY
or
INTELLIGENCE SUMMARY.
(Erase heading not required.)

Instructions regarding War Diaries and Intelligence Summaries are contained in F. S. Regs., Part II. and the Staff Manual respectively. Title pages will be prepared in manuscript.

Place	Date	Hour	Summary of Events and Information	Remarks and references to Appendices
NORTLEULINGHEM	Dec 24		Bathing.	
	25		The Battⁿ attended Divine Service on the Battⁿ Parade Ground. Reinforcements 1 Officer CAPT^N G. RICHARDS and 1 O.R.	
	26		No Parades. Football. Demobilization. 44 O.R.S. proceeded to Dispersal Camps.	
	27		Bathing. Working on New Camp.	
	28		2 Coys working on New Camp.	
	29		Battⁿ attended Church Parade in Church of Hut at 11-15 hours. Demobilization 10 O.R. 2 Coys at 10-30 hours and reassemble at P 12 b & fired 2 Coys proceeded to Range at P 12 b & fired Rapid-mag + Casuals. The other half Battⁿ working on New Camp.	
	30			
	31		Bathing. 2 Coys working on New Camp.	

A. Barrett Lieut
for
A. Col. Commanding
4th Battⁿ North Staffs Reg^t.

WAR DIARY
or
INTELLIGENCE SUMMARY.
(Erase heading not required.)

Army Form C. 2118.

4 N Staff

Instructions regarding War Diaries and Intelligence Summaries are contained in F. S. Regs., Part II. and the Staff Manual respectively. Title pages will be prepared in manuscript.

Place	Date	Hour	Summary of Events and Information	Remarks and references to Appendices
WORTLEULLINGHEM			The Brigadier Jujurat expected 2 C.O.s at 10.00 hours. 2 C.O.s working on General Corps Demobilization. 3 O.R.s proceeded to Dispersal Camp.	
WORTLEULLINGHEM	Jan 2		The Battalion paraded in full strength on Battalion parade ground under its Commanding Officer, Lt. Colonel Mackie at 10.00 hours. The C.O. went forward to the Dalton to the Junior C.O. The C.O. column had at the Battalion column 15 + namely the company commanders viz:- Capt. W.H. Bird M.C., Lieut. H. Ronald, G.S.M. M. Bateman, Sergt-Major Williams D.C.M. & Sergt. R.E. Woodcock M.M. Demobilization 2 O.R. proceeded to Dispersal Camp.	
WORTLEULLINGHEM	Jan 3		Letters A and B C.O.s continued work on New Contract. The Battalion paraded C C.O.s took the field and B.O.s D.C.s up D.C.s 10.30 A.M. o. C C.O.s 15 to Demobilisation. 3 O.R. proceeded to Dispersal Camp.	
WORTLEULLINGHEM	Jan 4		The Battalion paraded on Battalion parade ground under the Commanding Officer at 10.0.0. hours for divine service and the Battalion paraded at 10.30 hours to Church Parade, which was held at Battalion parade ground.	
WORTLEULLINGHEM	Jan 5		The Right half Battalion paraded on Battalion parade ground for divine service in the Belgian Chapel. Paraded at 10.30 hours. Church service at 11.15 hours.	

WAR DIARY
or
INTELLIGENCE SUMMARY.
(Erase heading not required.)

Army Form C. 2118.

Place	Date	Hour	Summary of Events and Information	Remarks and references to Appendices
MONTIGNY-LE-TILLEUL	7th		The Battalion proceeded to Range at 10 a.m. for an inspection of marching-in (winter) and contents of the packs which was satisfactory. The afternoon was spent on the reorganisation of the Companies.	
	8th		Demolition of Defence Camp. O.C. Letter "B" proceeded to Defence Camp and LETTER "A" and LETTER "B" Coys proceeded (in lorries) at 09.00 hours to LETTER "A" and LETTER "C" Coys Continued work on General. The troops at MONNEGOUE were changed to the Battalion.	
APPLANCHETTE	9th		LETTER "A" and LETTER "C" Coys demolition operations were carried out by Q.C. and continued by LETTER "B" LETTER "D" Coy proceeded to relieve carried on work on OMI Demolition.	
MONTIGNY-LE-TILLEUL	9th		The completion teams proceeded to many of P.O.W. to render any assistance possible. LETTERS A & C Coys continued demolition & completion and OR's proceeded to new camp. Demolition and training new carried on by the entering Coys, one letter later carried on by the Battalion.	
MONTE SUIR EN MONT	10th		The Commander Senior inspected Rifles & Service Arms of the Battalion. LETTERS "B" & "D" Coys continued work on new camp. The troops at MONNEGOUE were ordered to the Battalion. Demolition to German Ranges invaded by Battalion cont.	

WAR DIARY
or
INTELLIGENCE SUMMARY.
(Erase heading not required.)

Army Form C. 2118.

Place	Date	Hour	Summary of Events and Information	Remarks and references to Appendices
	Jan 11th		The Battalion landed at 0930 hours for ceremonial march with the Canadian Officials. The following officers attended the Parade – Genl. Sir. S. Sandys, Lt. E.B. Beeson & Lt. Col. Donaldson & O.C. Parade.	
			13 disposed Camp	
	Jan 12th		The night before Battalion paraded for Divine Service in the Crunch Army Hut at 10.30; the C.O. & C.O.F. paraded at 11.15	
	Jan 13th		The teams competing in the Divisional Rifle Meeting fired on the range at P.12.B. The Lewis Gun range in P.5.a. was allotted to "A" Coy. "A" & "C" Companies provided working parties on the site of the new camp. The Battalion Pump Troupe performed in the Crunch Army Hut during the evening.	
	Jan 14th		"B" Coy Companies provided working parties on the site of the new camp. The baths of MONNECOVE were allotted to the Battalion 2/Lt L. Peculs was transferred from "A" Coy to "C" Coy.	

WAR DIARY
or
INTELLIGENCE SUMMARY.
(Erase heading not required.)

Army Form C. 2118.

Place	Date	Hour	Summary of Events and Information	Remarks and references to Appendices
	Jan 15th		The Battn paraded for Inspection by the Brigadier General who was very pleased with the turnout	
	16th		Lewis Gun practice was carried out on the Range at P.S.a. Each Coy paraded 1 Offr & 30 O.Rs for work on the Gun Camp. Demobilization, 9 O.Rs proceeded to Dispersal Camp.	
	17th		Battn paraded at full strength under the Commanding Officer for Ceremonial Drill.	
	18th		The Battn paraded at full strength on the Battn Parade Ground to receive the Colours on their arrival from LICHFIELD where they had been deposited in the Cathedral for the period of the War. Numerous Officers from different Units in the Division were present for the ceremony, including Brigadier General A.J. TURNER. CMG. DSO. Lt Col. JOHNSON DSO. & Major HOBSON. The Kings Colour was carried by Lt W.H. BIRD. M.C. and the Regimental Colour by Lt T.H. BARRETT, the escort consisting	

WAR DIARY
or
INTELLIGENCE SUMMARY.
(Erase heading not required.)

Army Form C. 2118.

Instructions regarding War Diaries and Intelligence Summaries are contained in F. S. Regs. Part II. and the Staff Manual respectively. Title pages will be prepared in manuscript.

Place	Date	Hour	Summary of Events and Information	Remarks and references to Appendices
			of Col. Sergt. Major M. BATEMAN, Sergt. W. JOHNSON, and Sergt. J.E. WOODCOCK. After the parade part the Brigadier made the following address to the Battn. "Col. Hall, Officers, W.O's, N.C.O.'s & Men of the 4th South Staffs Regt. Your colours are again entrusted to your safeguard, after having been away while the Batt. has been on active service. They are truly a sacred emblem for the rally round. In olden days a rallying point was given in battle, & the colours were always that rallying point, and many is the occasion in the glorious annals of British history that men have sacrificed their lives to safeguard the colours. Modern warfare does not permit the colours now being taken up in action, but you can never the less safeguard them by your devotion to point of loyalty. I have no doubt that the colours	

A6945 Wt. W1422/M1160 350,000 12/16 D. D. & L. Forms/C./2118/14.

WAR DIARY
or
INTELLIGENCE SUMMARY.
(Erase heading not required.)

Army Form C. 2118.

Place	Date	Hour	Summary of Events and Information	Remarks and references to Appendices
	Jan		are safe in the keeping of the Battalion."	
	19th		Demobilization. 6 O.R's proceeded to Dispersal Camp. The Batt'n attached Divge Stores on the Church Army Hut. Right Half Batt'n at 10.30 hours. Left Half Batt'n at 11-15 hours.	
	20th		The Range at P12d was allotted for the use of the Completion Team, & the Range at P5a for Lewis Gun Practice. The usual working party was provided for the Jew Camp.	
	21st		Demobilization. 6 O.R's proceeded to Dispersal Camp. Working party provided for the Jew Camp. The bye proceeded in turn to the Baths at MONICOVE CAMP. Lewis Gun practice on Range at P5 a.	
	22nd		Manual working party on Jew Camp. & Lewis Gun practice on Range P5 a	
	23rd		Working Party on Jew Camp. Lewis gun practice at Range P5 a. & Working party on Jew Camp.	
	24th		Batt'n paraded for Medical Inspection. 10 O.R's to Dispersal Camp	

WAR DIARY or INTELLIGENCE SUMMARY

Army Form C. 2118.

Place	Date	Hour	Summary of Events and Information	Remarks and references to Appendices
	24		also 1 Officer. Bathing Team for training & work on New Camp. Demobilization. 9 O.R's proceeded to Dispersal Camp	
	25		The Batt'n attended Divine Service in Church. Hut.	
	26		Demobilization. 9 O.R's proceeded to the Dispersal Camp. Completion Team proceeded on Range P.12. Work on New Camp. 2 Officers & 14 O.R's proceeded to Dispersal Camp for Demobilization.	
	27		Work on New Camp. A Team proceeded to Range at P.12 to fire preliminary rounds for the Hh. Competition at 85 Div. Rifle Meeting, but on their arrival at the Range they found the Meeting postponed & received orders to return to Camp as the Batt'n had received orders to stand to."	
	28		Lieut. H. BARRETT proceeded to CALAIS with the advance party to make any necessary arrangements	

WAR DIARY
or
INTELLIGENCE SUMMARY.
(Erase heading not required.)

Army Form C. 2118.

Place	Date	Hour	Summary of Events and Information	Remarks and references to Appendices
	July 28		The Battⁿ proceeded to CALAIS by 50th^{tn} Ferry arriving at No 3 Leave Camp BEAUMARIS at 20.30 hours. Tea had been provided for the Officers & after this had been served they resumed the Lorries & the Battⁿ proceeded to No 6 Leave Camp West where Headquarters were made.	
CALAIS	29th		Owing to strikes trouble was expected from the Troops in No 6 Leave Camp East, so the Battⁿ provided piquets for 4 Bridges over the Canal leading to H.Q. 22 A.D. The position was very unpleasant for crowds formed on the Bridges & as they were not allowed to cross, a few ringleaders tried to persuade them. Fortunately they were unsuccessful & when the Battⁿ was relieved by the 15th Sherwood Foresters the situation was fairly quiet. Relief was complete by 18.00 hrs	
	30		The Battⁿ remained at No 6 Leave Camp West. Letters & Pay	

Army Form C. 2118.

WAR DIARY
or
INTELLIGENCE SUMMARY.
(Erase heading not required.)

Place	Date	Hour	Summary of Events and Information	Remarks and references to Appendices
	31st 30		At 10.30 hours the Batt paraded to force an entry into 306 Camp East. A & B Coys moved first & on arriving on position they prepared to Road between the Leave Camp & the Camp occupied by the Labour Corps, according to orders. The other 2 Coys moved up & to the same road. The whole operation was carried out by the 35th Division and by 12.00 hours the ringleaders had been arrested & the remainder of the men transferred to 304 Camp, from which Camp they proceeded to rejoin their Units. The operations were very successful, & all risks were pleased that bloodshed had been avoided. On returning to Camp, B Coy acted as Flying Piquet. Situation Quiet. Troops remained in Billets.	

A.Barrett Lieut
for
O.C. 4 South Staffs.

4th N Stafordshire Regt

Army Form C. 2118.

WAR DIARY
or
INTELLIGENCE SUMMARY.

98/14

Place	Date	Hour	Summary of Events and Information	Remarks and references to Appendices
CALAIS	Feb 1919 1		Clearing up camp etc	
	2		Do.	
	3		The Batt moved from BEAUMARIS CAMP. Batt Headquarters and Right Half Battalion marching to FONTINETTES STATION where they entrained for MARQUISE, and the LEFT Half Batt under Capt A. Hassock S.C. to CALAIS DUNES STATION, where they entrained for ZENEGHEM. The 1st Line Transport moved by road under Brigade arrangements. On arrival at MARQUISE the Right Half Batt marched to LES BARDES where billets were ready.	
	4		Demobilization. 20 O.Rs proceeded to Dispersal Camp. Escorts provided for Prisoners of War. Demobilization 2 Offrs & 20 O.Rs proceeded to the Dispersal Camp.	
	5		Escorts provided for P.O.W. Demobilization 1 Off & 12 O.Rs proceeded to Dispersal Camp.	

Army Form C. 2118.

WAR DIARY
or
INTELLIGENCE SUMMARY.
(Erase heading not required.)

Place	Date	Hour	Summary of Events and Information	Remarks and references to Appendices
LES BARDES	1919 Jan 6th		Escorts provided for P.O.W. Demobilization. 22 O.Rs proceeded to Dispersal Camp.	
	7		Escorts for P.O.W.	
	8		Escorts for P.O.W. Demobilization. 21 O.Rs proceeded to Dispersal Camp	
	9		The Right Half Batt'n attended Divine Service in the Y.S.C.A. Hut at LES BARDES	
	10		Escorts for P.O.W. Demobilization. 10 O.Rs proceeded to Dispersal Camp	
	11		Escorts for P.O.W.	
	12		Do	
	13		Do	
	14		Escorts provided for P.O.W. Demobilization 4 O.Rs proceeded to Dispersal Camp.	
	15		Escorts provided for P.O.W. Demobilization. 1 O.R. proceeded to Dispersal Camp.	

Army Form C. 2118.

WAR DIARY
or
INTELLIGENCE SUMMARY.
(Erase heading not required.)

Instructions regarding War Diaries and Intelligence Summaries are contained in F. S. Regs., Part II. and the Staff Manual respectively. Title pages will be prepared in manuscript.

Place	Date 1919	Hour	Summary of Events and Information	Remarks and references to Appendices
LES BARDES	Feb. 16"		Right Half Battⁿ attached Divis^e Service in the of G.C.A. Hd^tQrt^s LES BARDES.	
	17		Escorts provided for P.O.W. Demobilization 10 O.R.^s proceeded to Disperse Camp.	
	18		Escorts provided for P.O.W.	
	19		Do Do	
	20		Do Do	
	21		Escorts provided for P.O.W. Demobilization 4 O.R^s proceeded to Disperse Camp.	
	22		Escorts provided for P.O.W. Demobilization 23 O.R.^s proceeded to Disperse Camp.	
	23		Right Half Battⁿ attached Divis^e Service in the G.H.Q.A. Hd^t Les Bardes. Demobilization 9 O.R^s proceeded to Dispersal Camp.	
	24		Escorts provided for P.O.W.	
	25		Do	

Army Form C. 2118.

WAR DIARY
or
INTELLIGENCE SUMMARY.
(Erase heading not required.)

Place	Date	Hour	Summary of Events and Information	Remarks and references to Appendices
Lo Bordes	Feb 26		Escorts provided for P.O.W. Coy.	
	27		Do	
	28		Do	
			HBennett Lieut	
			for	
			O.C. 4th North Stafford Regt	

Army Form C. 2118.

WAR DIARY
or
INTELLIGENCE SUMMARY.
(Erase heading not required.)

4 M Staff
4 Mch 18

Place	Date	Hour	Summary of Events and Information	Remarks and references to Appendices
Les Baraques	March 1st		Escorts provided for P.O.W. Coys. Issuing etc.	
	2nd		The Bn attached Divge Service as the Y.B.C.A. Hut at 10.45 hours. Demobilisation of 2.6.R's proceeded to the Dispersal Camp.	
	3rd		Escorts provided for P.O.W. Coys.	
	4th		Escorts for P.O.W. Coys. Demobilisation. 2 6 R's proceeded to the Dispersal Camp.	
	5th		B.H.Q. A & B Coys moved by rail to Beaugaires Camp. Calais. The labour were carried by 2nd Lts E.B. Williams & 2/Lt J. Dutton.	
BEAUMARIS	6th		Inspection of kit & clothing etc.	
	7th		Escorts provided for P.O.W.	
	8th		Do Do	
	9th		Voluntary Divine Services held in the Church Army Hut at 10.00 hrs. Demobilisation 2 6 R's proceeded to Dispersal Camp.	

Army Form C. 2118.

WAR DIARY
or
INTELLIGENCE SUMMARY.
(Erase heading not required.)

Instructions regarding War Diaries and Intelligence Summaries are contained in F. S. Regs., Part II, and the Staff Manual respectively. Title pages will be prepared in manuscript.

Place	Date	Hour	Summary of Events and Information	Remarks and references to Appendices
BEAULMARIS	March 10		Inspection of Kit Clothing & Rifles	
	11		Escorts provided for P.O.W. Cys.	
	12		Do.	
	13		Do.	
	14		Do.	
	15		Do.	
	16		Voluntary Services held in the Church Army Hut. 1 Offr Lt. J.M. SKEAFF proceeded to Dispersal Camp	
	17		Escorts for P.O.M. Cys. Bathing	
	18		Escorts for P.O.M. Cys	
	19		Do.	
	20		Do.	
	21		Do.	
	22		Do.	
	23		Voluntary Divine Services held in the Church Army Hut	

WAR DIARY
or
INTELLIGENCE SUMMARY.
(Erase heading not required.)

Army Form C. 2118.

Place	Date	Hour	Summary of Events and Information	Remarks and references to Appendices
BEAUMARIS	March 24		Escorts provided for P.O.W. Coys.	
	25		B.H.Q. A & B Coys moved by rail to ST. OMER & from there marched to the old camp at NORTLEULINGHEM. LT H. BARRETT carried the Kings Colour 2LT S.E. JENKINS carried the Regt Colour. C & D Coys marched from ZENEGHEM to NORTLEULINGHEM. Demobilization 28 O.Rs proceeded to the Dispersal Camp.	
NORTLEULINGHEM	26		The Batn paraded under Major H. MEREDITH at 10.00hr for inspection with LT A. HODGSON D.C.M. in attendance. Capt. W.T. LERWAY appointed Off in charge of Byros. Byros & Camp sanitation. A Standing Board assembled to investigate the P.R.I. Offrs & Pro Bus Canteen & Imprest accounts, consisting of Capt G. RICHARDS President, Capt H. HENSTOCK M.C. & Capt W.A. BIRD M.C. members.	

Army Form C. 2118.

WAR DIARY
or
INTELLIGENCE SUMMARY.
(Erase heading not required.)

Instructions regarding War Diaries and Intelligence Summaries are contained in F. S. Regs., Part II. and the Staff Manual respectively. Title pages will be prepared in manuscript.

Place	Date	Hour	Summary of Events and Information	Remarks and references to Appendices
	March 27th		The Battn paraded under the Adjt. at 11-30 hrs for Drill.	
	28th		The Battn paraded under the Adjt. at 11-30 hrs for Drill. The following award has been approved. 235266 Corpl. A. BOULDEN. Belgian Decoration Militaire 2nd Class & CROIX de GUERRE. Demobilization. 6 O.R.s proceeded to the Dispersal Camp. MAJOR. H. MEREDITH. assumes command of 4th Battn South Staffs Regt. vice Lt. Col. D.M.B. HALL. D.S.O. to Brigade Command.	
	29		Trevor Inspections Cleaning. Battn Sports were held on the Battn Parade Ground.	
	30		The Battn attended Divine Service in the General Army Hut at 10.30 hrs	

Army Form C. 2118.

WAR DIARY
or
INTELLIGENCE SUMMARY.
(Erase heading not required.)

Place	Date	Hour	Summary of Events and Information	Remarks and references to Appendices
	March 30		Captn. H.B. MOSER appointed Acting Adjutant vice Captn C.S. DYE M.C. who proceeded to U.K. en route for ARCHANGEL	
	31		Training & recreation	

H. Barrett Lieut
for
O.C. 4 North Staffs Regt.

4th N. Stafford Regt:

To:- D.A.G.
      3rd Echelon.
        B.E.F. France

9

Herewith War Diary of the 4th Batt: N. Stafford Regt: from 1/4/19 to 24/4/19, being the date of arrival in England.

          H.B. Moser,
          Capt & Adjt:
     for.
  Lieut: Col: Cmdg 4th N. Stafford Regt:

RIPON
26/4/19

WAR DIARY
or
INTELLIGENCE SUMMARY.
(Erase heading not required.)

Army Form C. 2118.

Place	Date	Hour	Summary of Events and Information	Remarks and references to Appendices
	April			
ROUTIEUVILINGHEM	1st		The Batts at EPERLECQUES were allotted to the Batt? Training and Recreation. The D.A.D.O.S. made his first official visit to the Batt? to examine the billy.......n therein + made complimentary remarks about the same.	
	2nd		Training and Recreation.	
	3rd		Training and Recreation.	
	4th		Training and Recreation. 2/Lt S.E. Jenkins appointed A.S.I. Adjutant vice Lt. H. Barrett who proceeded to U.K. for demobilization, to date from 1/4/19. The following officers left for demobilization:- Capt W.T. LERWAY, Lt H. BARRETT, 2/Lt B.C. WOOD, 2/Lt J. DUTTON, 2/Lt L. PEARSE, 2/Lt W.R. BRACEY.	
	5th		Training & Recreation.	
	6th		Recreation.	
	7th		Recreation.	
	8th		The Coffs at EPERLECQUES were allotted to the Batt? Recreation	

Army Form C. 2118.

WAR DIARY
or
INTELLIGENCE SUMMARY.
(Erase heading not required.)

Instructions regarding War Diaries and Intelligence Summaries are contained in F. S. Regs., Part II. and the Staff Manual respectively. Title pages will be prepared in manuscript.

Place	Date	Hour	Summary of Events and Information	Remarks and references to Appendices
NORTLEULINGHAM	9th		Training & Recreation	
	10th		Training & Recreation. Capt J.T. Hughes R.A.M.C. left the Battalion for duty at No. 10 C.C.S. I.O.R. for Dispersal Camp.	
	11th		Training & Recreation.	
	12th		The Battalion was for chan w/s. Major H. MEREDITH 2/Lt S. WILLIAMS & Pte F. Carp with 74 O.R's. were transferred to No. 278 P.O.W. Coy meet ALBERT. Capt H. HENSTOCK M.C. 2/Lt E.A. REEVES. 2/Lt J.F.B. ELLISON with 73 O.R's. were transferred to No. 235 P.O.W. Coy meet CAMBRAI. 74. P.F.M. WILLIAMS 2/Lt F.E. CORP 2/Lt S. GOODYER with 69 O.R's. were transferred to No. 239 P.D.W. Coy meet ACHEUX. Capt G. RICHARDS with 74 O.R's was transferred to No. 292 P.O.W Coy meet BERTRY.	
	13th		The Battalion moved off at 8.00 hours to WATTEN STATION to entrain. The Cadre was left behind. Training & Recreation.	
	14th		Training & Recreation	

WAR DIARY
or
INTELLIGENCE SUMMARY.

(Erase heading not required.)

Army Form C. 2118.

Place	Date	Hour	Summary of Events and Information	Remarks and references to Appendices
NORTHULINGHAM	15th		Training & Recreation	
	16th		Training & Recreation	
	17th		Training & Recreation	
	18th		Recreation	
	19th		The Cadre left NORTHULINGHAM (6 staff) for ENGLAND, marched to ST OMER & entrained there.	
	20th		The Cadre arrived at DUNKIRK at 01.30 a.m. & spent the day in camp.	
	21st		The Cadre boarded the ship & embarked itself to sleep on the boat.	
	22nd		The Cadre sailed for RITON at 05.00 hours on H.M.S. VICATAH. The Cadre consisted of 2/Lieut. D.M.B. HALL D.S.O. Commanding Officer, Capt. H.B. MOSER, Adjutant, 2/Lieut. A. HODGSON, Quarter Master, 2/Lieut. S.E. JENKINS, Lewis Gun Officer, & also 32 O.R's. Also 2/Lieut W.J. HOLLINGSWORTH who carried the King's Colour and 2/Lieut. K.R. BRAIN who carried the Regimental Colour. Arrived Southampton. S.E. Jenkins 2/Lieut A/59/Adj for Lieut. Col. Comdg. 1st N. Stafford Regt.	

www.ingramcontent.com/pod-product-compliance
Lightning Source LLC
Chambersburg PA
CBHW081556160426
43191CB00011B/1950